BEFORE YOU FLY AWAY

life lessons from home

Christina Geist

Designed by Todd True

Copyright © 2025 Christina Geist

All rights reserved.

ISBN: 979-8-9929817-1-1

AUTHOR'S NOTE

For the kids out there spreading your wings, making your way in the world, and leaving a loving adult behind, this book is for you.

For the grownups out there waving from doorways, looking back on millions of little moments, and wondering if you taught them the big, important stuff along the way, this book is for you. So is this hug. Can you feel it? Good.

For Lucie and George, before you fly away, this book is for you.

This is a collection of life lessons. Some big. Some small. Some were learned the hard way, others by observation, while several are still a work in progress. Lesson number one, after all, is to be nice to yourself.

With Love, Cg

1

Be nice to yourself.

2

Use your words.

They are your superpower.

Take care of your space.

Take care of your things.

Take care of your body.

3

You only get one.

4

It's really cool to be smart.

5

A good leader

is a great listener.

6

Make eye contact.

Conflict begins in your mind.

7

Resolving it begins there, too.

8

Appreciate your blessings,

out loud,

in real time.

9

Open your mind

before you

open your mouth.

Don't expect people

to be perfect.

10

Don't be surprised

when they're not.

11

Use your gifts to create memories with the people you love.

12

Order dessert.

With a scoop of vanilla.

13

Don't make big decisions when you're exhausted.

14

Respect people

who are doing their job.

No matter the job.

Positive thoughts

are like fireflies.

Let them out so they

can do their magic.

16

Laughing at yourself

is not the same

as putting yourself

down.

17

Costume parties are more fun.

18

Walk outdoors,

in every season.

19

You will break a heart.

Someone will break yours.

When it happens,

I will be here.

20

There are no fairy godmothers

in the real world.

You alone have the power

to change your path.

21

Smile at people in passing.

Say good morning.

Hold the door.

22

Trim your nails.

Introduce yourself again.

23

Nine times out of ten,

they forgot your name, too.

24

Recklessness and regret

go hand in hand.

25

Every job you have

is an education.

26

Your life is measured in

your relationships,

not your accomplishments.

27

Gossip is like gold.

People simply cannot resist flashing it around.

28

Your phone is not a substitute for a real-life friend when walking home at night.

I trust you.

Unless you give me

a reason not to.

30

If your jokes rely on making fun of other people, you're not actually funny.

31

Don't set an alarm

if you don't need one.

32

A compliment should be sincere, and it should be shared.

33

Think two steps ahead.

Anticipate.

Prepare.

34

Leave the day behind you

and read a book

before you fall asleep.

35

Making friends is like playing with magnets.

Some attract.

Some don't. Let it be.

36

Safety first.

Zero exceptions.

Don't talk someone

out of the compliment

they just gave you.

Accept it. Own it.

38

I will love you

no matter what you do.

Others may not always

be able to.

39

If you spend your time coveting other people's stuff, you will never be satisfied.

40

Even the best people you know are capable of making terrible choices.

41

If there's no laughter between you, something's wrong.

42

Figure it out.

You're 100% capable.

43

If relationships were simple, there would be no music, movies, TV shows or theater.

44

Rinsing something

is not the same as washing it.

45

The only thing

we know for sure about life

is that it won't last forever.

Stay up

and watch the sunrise.

You can sleep

on the plane home.

Beautiful people with beautiful things will attract attention. What they do with that attention is what makes them interesting, or not.

If your cup is full in life,

pour something positive into

someone else's.

Life is lived in chapters.

49

If you are sad when a

chapter ends and it's time

to turn the page,

it means you did it right.

50

Call home.

We need to hear your voice.

CHRISTINA GEIST is the *New York Times* bestselling children's book author of *Sorry Grown-Ups, You Can't Go to School!*, *Buddy's Bedtime Battery* and *Buddy's New Buddy*. This is her first book for big kids. She lives in New York with her husband, Willie, and their children, Lucie and George.

TODD TRUE is a professor of graphic design, the award-winning designer of corporate and brand logos including BP and John Deere, and a globally recognized creative director across industries. He lives in Pennsylvania with his wife, Lisa, and their children, Austin, Jett and Ruby.

Christina and Todd have been writing & design partners for 20 years. For more about their branding work for clients big and small, visit TrueGeist.com.